How to Seize the Transfer of Wealth

by
Dennis Burke

Dennis Burke Publications

Unless otherwise indicated, all Scripture quotations are taken from the *New King James Version*.

The Amplified Bible © The Lockman Foundation, La Habra, California, 1954, 1958.

New Living Translation © 1996. Tyndale House Publishers, Inc., Wheaton, Illinois.

The Holy Bible, New King James Version © 1982. Thomas Nelson, Inc., Nashville, Tennessee.

The Holy Bible © Oxford University Press, London, England.

The New Testament in Modern English by J. B. Phillips © 1961, The MacMillian Company, New York, New York.

The Blessings of Obedience © 1984. Whitaker House, Pittsburgh, Pennsylvania.

How to Seize the Transfer of Wealth
ISBN 1-890026-10-7
© 2000 by Dennis Burke
P. O. Box 150043
Arlington, TX 76015

TABLE OF CONTENTS

1 Our Covenant of Increase 7

2 Creating an Atmosphere
   for Increase 19

3 Rising Above Average
   into Super-abundance 31

4 Positioned for God's Transfer
   of Wealth 43

5 Cutting the Root of the
   Enemy's Power 55

6 Move Toward Your Dream
   by Blessing the Blessed 65

7 The Power to Prosper in
   All Things 77

God's thoughts are
fixed on you! He is
looking for ways to bring
His best and His
increase in your life.
The New Covenant places
you in a position to receive all
of God's goodness
and provision.

Chapter One

Our Covenant
of Increase

To the person who understands the idea of covenant, it is no mystery that the New Covenant brings all the blessings of God into the life of the believer. It places you in a position to receive all of God's goodness and provision.

The strength of a covenant brings two parties together and gives us access into one another's wealth and influence. Really, we have nothing to offer God, but He has everything to offer us. We receive His strength and richness, and He takes our weakness and lack.

As the focus of God's love, you have been brought into this covenant by simple faith in the sacrifice of Jesus, and have been given the right to receive all that this covenant includes.

It is important to realize that you must provide the avenues for God to bring His plan to you. He is the source of the provision and miracles, but your obedience, your faith and your faithfulness to Him are the pathways that bring His abundance to you.

The more you understand how God thinks about you, the easier it is to be obedient and stand in faith on His Word. Psalm 115 gives us powerful insight into the way God thinks:

> The Lord has been mindful of us; He will bless us; He will bless the house of Israel; He will bless the house of Aaron. He will bless those who fear the Lord, both small and great. May the Lord give you increase more and more, you and your children. May you be blessed by the Lord, Who made heaven and earth. The heaven, even the heavens, are the Lord's; but the earth He has given to the children of men (verses 12-16).

God's thoughts are fixed on you! He has remembered you. He has not forgotten you or the things you are facing. God is looking for ways to bring His best and His increase into your life.

The verses from Psalm 115 tell us that God not only has us on His mind, but increase as well. He is the giver of all good and perfect things and He desires to bring increase to you.

> Every good gift and every perfect gift is from above, and comes down from the Father of lights, with whom there is no variation or shadow of turning (James 1:17).

He Will Bless You

Whenever we speak about covenants, we must always look back to the covenant between God and Abram.

One of the first things God spoke to Abram was: "I will bless you." These words have been at the very heart of God's desire for all men and women. He is a giver and is committed to bringing His blessings to His people.

In establishing His covenant with Abram, God clearly stated what He would do for Abram through this agreement.

Notice what is says in Genesis 12:1-3:

Now the Lord had said to Abram: "Get out of your country, from your family and from your father's house, to a land that I will show you. I will make you a great nation; I will bless you and make your name great; and you shall be a blessing. I will bless those who bless you, and I will curse him who curses you; and in you all the families of the earth shall be blessed."

The Amplified Bible says it this way: "I will make of you a great nation, and I will bless you with abundant increase of favors." God *wants* to bless and favor *you*.

Abundant Increase of the Favor of God

Think about that: abundant increase of the favor of God. God considered it such a priority for His blessings and increase to be brought to mankind. He declared that it would be the first thing He would do for Abram—if he would only obey God.

As Abram began to obey God and to walk with Him, he saw the power of His covenant in action. Abram would immediately see the increase that the covenant brought him.

Genesis 13:6 records the abundance that Abram and his nephew, Lot, received from the Lord:

> Now the land was not able to support
> them, that they might dwell together,
> for their possessions were so great that
> they could not dwell together.

Their *possessions* had increased abundantly. It was more than they could contain as long as they lived together. In order for Abram to continue increasing, he would need to go on with God and be separated from Lot.

The covenant brought an increase of possessions, but there would be more; God said He would give Abram land as far as his eyes could see. He would give Abram descendants and land and increase of wealth as well as influence, all because he would continue to live by faith in the covenant between him and God Almighty.

God and Abraham—God and You

Abram is called the father of faith. He walked in the kind of faith that is a model to all generations—the faith that pleased God. He believed that his covenant with God would bring Him increase, and for the rest of his life, he saw that increase come to him.

In Genesis 17, God again spoke to Abram regarding His covenant. It was at this time that God changed his name from Abram to Abraham. God established the way the covenant was to work and declared that He would "multiply him exceedingly."

God continued to increase Abraham in land, cattle, descendants and wealth. He experienced God causing him to prosper in all aspects of his life.

When you begin to understand this covenant relationship between God and Abraham, you can comprehend *your* relationship with God to a greater degree, because you are the "seed of Abraham."

Galatians 3:29 says, "And if you are Christ's, then you are Abraham's seed, and heirs according to the promise."

Therefore, the better you understand how God blessed Abraham, the better you will understand your own position in Him.

Blessing or Materialism?

For too long the Body of Christ has struggled with the realization that God wants to bring increase and even financial miracles into our lives. There seems to be an underlying fear that to want God to bring any kind of material increase was to be *materialistic.*

This fear of financial increase as a part of the blessing of God has been fed by people who have a misconception of God Himself.

To be materialistic means *to endeavor to satisfy an emotional or spiritual need with a physical thing.* No devoted believer wants to have material things in a place of priority over God. God wants you to increase materially as long as *you possess* the things, but *they* do not *possess* you.

When King David fell to his darkest moment through adultery and murder, God spoke to him and said,

> I anointed you king over Israel, and I delivered you from the hand of Saul. I gave you your master's house and your master's wives into your keeping, and gave you the house of Israel and Judah. *And if that had been too little, I also would have given you much more!* (2 Samuel 12:7-8).

God did not rebuke David by telling him he had too much. David had sinned, but it was not the wealth or power that was the problem. God was ready and willing to increase him even further if that was what David had wanted.

God does not want to withhold His abundance from you, but you must walk with Him and honor His Word for the promise of increase to come to you.

The Miracle of Abundance

God again reveals His attitude toward abundance with the very first miracle Jesus performed. The miracle at Cana, in which Jesus multiplied the wine, was a miracle of abundance.

It was during a wedding feast in Cana, and the host had run out of wine to serve his guests. Jesus' mother told Him about the problem and then instructed the servants of the host by saying, "Whatever He says to you, do it" (John 2:5). Verse 11 further states, "This beginning of signs Jesus did in Cana of Galilee, and manifested His glory; and His disciples believed in Him."

God's glory was revealed through a miracle that did not heal anyone, nor did it deliver anyone from demonic power. It was a miracle of abundance. Jesus did what He saw His Father do; He provided abundant supply—*increase!*

It is *significant* that the first miracle was a miracle of abundance. God has made a clear case that blessing and increase are a major part of His plan for His people.

Just as Abraham believed God's first words that He would bless him through His covenant, you also must receive His promise and His plan by faith, and activate it in your life.

Establishing His Covenant

Look closely again at Psalm 115:16: "The heaven, even the heavens, are the Lord's; but the earth He has given to the children of men."

The wealth of the earth is not for those who are living for greed, lust or selfishness. It is reserved for those who walk with God and have put Him first in their life.

The world has misused wealth and its power for ungodly or personal gain, and not the purpose for which God gave it.

Wealth and riches are given to us for the pur-

15

pose of establishing the covenant of God. Deuteronomy 8:18 says,

> And you shall remember the Lord your
> God, for it is He who gives you power
> to get wealth, that He may establish
> His covenant which He swore to your
> fathers, as it is this day.

God gives you the power to get wealth. His wisdom and anointing empower you to possess the wealth and riches for the purpose of establishing—*to set up, ordain or to prove*—His covenant.

God made a covenant with Abraham, and re-established it with Isaac and Jacob. In that covenant, He promised to bless and multiply them and their seed. God is bound to His Word, and therefore He is bound to bring that increase into your life if you will walk with Him by faith.

It is time for the increase of the people of God to be "exceedingly abundantly above all that we ask or think" (Ephesians 3:20). It is the day for increase to come and the message of faith in God to flourish among God's people.

How to Seize the Transfer of Wealth

As you increase, you are able to use that wealth to further establish God's Covenant in others. The ultimate purpose for your increase is not so that you can squander it on yourself, but that the message and power of God's Covenant may be brought to all people—worldwide.

Lay hold on your covenant and God will establish His Covenant of increase in you.

These are the days of the

outpouring of God's presence

and the moving of God's Spirit

in a greater measure than

at anytime in history. He is

bringing increase to His

people in every dimension of life.

Chapter Two

Creating an Atmosphere for Increase

The picture of a farmer sowing seed appears frequently in Scripture as an example of the believer sowing the seeds of God's Word. James 5:7-8 uses the farmer to help us understand the attitude that will bring increase in this present day.

> Therefore be patient, brethren, until the coming of the Lord. See how the farmer waits for the precious fruit of the earth, waiting patiently for it until it receives the early and latter rain.
>
> You also be patient. Establish your hearts, for the coming of the Lord is at hand.

The signs of the times indicate that the return

of Jesus Christ is near. I believe that this is the final generation. But whether or not this is the world's final generation, this is certainly *your* final generation!

We must be busy about our Father's business. James shows us the farmer sows his seed and then looks hopefully for the coming of the rain that will cause it to grow.

Expect a Great Harvest

Patience is not merely inactive waiting. The Bible explanation of the word patience is to continue unmoved by any attack or evidence that is contrary to God's promises.

The farmer is not idle as he waits for the rain to come. He is busy attending to the field. He works hard not only sowing the seed, but also to keep a quality environment in which it can flourish.

His expectation is for a great harvest, and all his work is done with that purpose in mind. Even though he knows that his time, money and effort will bring no income until harvest time, his confidence in the future crop inspires him to continue.

In Philippians 1:19-20 the Apostle Paul speaks of this kind of expectation.

20

For I know that this will turn out for my deliverance through your prayer and the supply of the Spirit of Jesus Christ, according to my earnest expectation and hope that in nothing I shall be ashamed, but with all boldness, as always, so now also Christ will be magnified in my body, whether by life or by death.

Notice he says that his deliverance is according to what he expects and hopes for. His expectation plays an important role in what he will receive.

Likewise, your expectation of God's Word becoming reality is vital to establishing His promises in your heart.

You expect to be healed, because you have found healing in God's Word. You expect prosperity and peace, because God has already provided it for every person who will receive.

An expectation is a strong anticipation. Our family dog is a Yorkshire terrier named Elliot. Like many dogs, when a dog biscuit is held in front of him, he knows the right thing to do.

He is certain that he will get the treat if he is

perfectly still and controlled. His eyes never leave the treat. He is focused and undistracted. His confidence is high—and although his nickname is Mr. Motion— he will remain still until he gets what he expects.

Intense expectation and hope work together hand in hand. Hope is a confident expectation. With an intense and confident expectation, you can look for the promises of God to become reality. Circumstances must not move your attention away. You must hold fast to what your faith in God's Word promises that you have received.

The farmer cannot stop and switch crops in the middle of the year. If there are difficult times, he must remain diligent in his work and confident that it will pay off in the end. He does everything in his power to keep the seed prepared for the rain.

Neither can the farmer change the weather conditions to make it rain. But this is where you, the believer, differ from the farmer, because there is something you can do to bring the Holy Spirit's rain onto your seed.

You can create an atmosphere for God's rain. Rain doesn't come out of a cloudless sky. Sometimes it doesn't even come out of a cloudy sky. Rain comes only when the atmospheric conditions are correct.

In the Bible, rain often represents the blessing and presence of God pouring onto His people. Hosea 6:3 says,

> Let us know, let us pursue the knowledge of the Lord. His going forth is established as the morning; He will come to us like the rain, like the latter and former rain to the earth.

Again in Ezekiel 34:26 it says,

> I will make them and the places all around My hill a blessing; and I will cause showers to come down in their season; there shall be showers of blessing.

These are the days of the outpouring of God's presence and the moving of God's Spirit in a greater measure than at any other time in history. God is opening the heavens to bring a flood of His goodness to humanity. He is bringing increase to His people in every dimension of life. You can flow with Him and see the rain of His anointing and presence in a deeper and more powerful way.

In Deuteronomy 11:13-14 are clear directions

in bringing a sustained increase of harvest.

> And it shall be that if you earnestly
> obey My commandments which I com-
> mand you today, to love the Lord your
> God and serve Him with all your heart
> and with all your soul, then I will give
> you the rain for your land in its sea-
> son, the early rain and the latter rain,
> that you may gather in your grain, your
> new wine, and your oil.

When the rain came to the land, increase ac-
companied it. The seed began to grow, as the rain
caused it to flourish.

Within the context of what God has said, His
people understood that the blessing would come if
they followed His instructions, and they would see
their material world increase as God brought His
blessing upon them.

Creating the Conditions for Blessing

The conditions for the blessing and outpouring
of the Spirit were created by the way the people
walked in the Word God had given them.

The instructions were clear. They centered on

a familiar but sometimes still uncomfortable word, *obedience*.

In order to obey God's Word, you must make it the first priority and final authority in your life. That means that you go to the Word first and believe His promise is true, regardless of contradicting evidence.

Obedience is going where He says to go and doing what He says to do. Isaiah 1:19 says, "If you are willing and obedient, you shall eat the good of the land."

The Word of God states over and over that there are blessings that come with obedience, but a penalty for disobedience. Many want the blessings yet do not want to obey. You must follow through with the instructions God gives, to receive the results He has promised.

If the believer is to be full of God's presence and experiencing His blessing, he must cultivate an attitude of obedience and a yielded heart toward God and His Word. Those who obey Him will best reveal His presence.

In his book, *The Blessing of Obedience*, Andrew Murray says, "Without obedience there cannot be the spiritual power to enter into the knowledge of

God's Word and will. Without obedience there cannot be the confidence, boldness, and liberty that knows that prayer is heard. Obedience is fellowship with God in His will. Without it there is no capacity for seeing, claiming, and holding the blessing He has for us."

If you will choose to follow the instructions in God's Word regarding your time, attitudes, giving, priorities and willingness to yield to His influence, you will create an atmosphere around you in which He can move.

The conflict is that there is an inner desire to please God and express our love to Him, and yet there remain outer influences and attitudes of independence that say, "I can do it on my own and still succeed."

Your willingness to pursue God's will increases as you discover the blessing of yielding your will to His.

It seems that one area most Christians struggle with is finances. In their hearts they want to be givers, and yet they have not realized that intentions without actions are equal to disobedience.

The Bible is clear about the giving that God

expects. He has a heart to give and has caused that desire to be born within you. Then He gives us the guidelines to follow for giving—tithes and offerings.

There is a vital link between a person's use of money and his or her life of obedience toward God. You can determine someone's priorities by observing how they spend their money. They put their money toward what they view as important.

You Invest in What You Value

You will invest in the thing that you value. When you value the advancing of the Gospel, you want to invest in the ministries that are promoting God's Word. When you hunger for real spiritual growth, you will spend time and money on tape or book materials that will cause you to grow.

Your giving into the Kingdom of God brings your personal financial world under His dominion. It is one way of demonstrating that Jesus is Lord over your life. When you give, you are giving a part of your life, because it took some of your life to earn that money.

Vikki and I have discovered over the years that as we honor God with our tithes and offerings, we are positioning ourselves for God's favor and increase to overtake us. It really is true!

Notice Proverbs 11:24-25:

There is one who scatters, yet increases more; and there is one who withholds more than is right but it leads to poverty. The generous soul will be made rich, and he who waters will also be watered himself.

Contrary to carnal thinking, your faithful giving—or scattering seed will bring increase to your life.

It takes a heart of faith and obedience to remain yielded to God. He will touch various areas of your life from finances to attitudes, and anything in between. But expectant obedience creates the atmosphere that will cause your seed to grow and His increase to become a reality.

The heart of God

is for you to rise above

the average into the

place where you are

super-abundantly supplied.

To fully bring this increase,

you must create the kind of

environment and atmosphere

that will bring the blessing

of God.

Chapter Three

Rising Above Average into Super-abundance

God has always wanted a covenant relationship with His people that would enable them to increase in every area of their lives.

In establishing covenant with Abraham, God made His thoughts clear.

> Now in Haran the Lord said to Abram, 'Go for yourself [for your own advantage] away from your country, from your relatives and your father's house, to the land that I will show you. And I will make of you a great nation, and I will bless you with abundant increase of favors and make your name famous and distinguished, and you will be a

blessing dispensing good to others' (Genesis 12:1-2, *The Amplified Bible*).

The heart of God is for you to rise above average into the place where you are super-abundantly
supplied. To fully bring this increase, you must create
the kind of environment and atmosphere that will
bring the blessing of God.

Deuteronomy 11:13-14 vividly illustrates how
you can bring the rain of God's blessing onto the
seed you have sown. Once that rain comes, your
seed will flourish.

> And it shall be that if you earnestly
> obey My commandments which I com-
> mand you today, to love the Lord your
> God and serve Him with all your heart
> and with all your soul, then I will give
> you the rain for your land in its season,
> the early rain and the latter rain, that
> you may gather in your grain, your new
> wine, and your oil.

Notice again the instructions: *obey*, *love* and
serve with your heart and your soul.

In looking at our love for God, we realize that

the only way we really love Him is to realize His love for us. First John 4:10 says, "In this is love, not that we loved God, but that He loved us and sent His Son to be the propitiation for our sins."

Love Without Conditions or Qualifications

His love for you is completely unconditional and without qualification. He loves you regardless of your commitment, your performance or your actions. He loves you whether or not you ever love Him.

For the person who has never experienced God's love, that kind of love is incomprehensible. Natural human love is so different. We love those who love us, while God loves without needing any response. But He expects His love to *create* a response. He has faith in His love and the response it will bring from those who receive it.

The covenant love of God is based not on an emotion but on the covenant relationship God has with man. In the Garden of Eden, there was a clear relationship that not even sin could destroy. After Adam sinned God entered the garden and sought His man once again.

Though they were driven out of the garden, God clothed Adam and Eve with the skin of an animal to cover their nakedness (Genesis 3:21). God would continue to love them, though they had destroyed the depth of their relationship with Him.

The New Covenant through Jesus has given access to a better relationship with God than Adam had in the garden. This love-covenant relationship will remove any inner wound or pain and any fear or weakness. It will restore the kind of fellowship your heavenly Father created you to enjoy with Him.

He has provided a way back into perfect fellowship with Him, even when we have sinned. First John 2:1 says, "And if anyone sins, we have an Advocate with the Father, Jesus Christ the righteous."

However, instead of resolving their failures through the free gift of forgiveness, many tend to do what Adam and Eve first did in the garden. They hid themselves and covered themselves with clothes they made from fig leaves.

A great deal of the misery we suffer comes from our continued attempts to hide and cover our weakness, and to compromise rather than confess our sin and receive forgiveness.

This covenant love that God has shown toward us is now within us. Romans 5:5 says, "The love of God has been poured out in our hearts by the Holy Spirit who was given to us."

Now we too are capable of loving without conditions. His divine love has freed us from the limits of human love alone.

When this is the foundation of a relationship or friendship, there is a strength that cannot be shaken. A marriage founded on this covenant love does not let difficulties and misunderstandings bring it to the brink of divorce. This commitment resolves incompatibility rather than tolerating it.

Love is a choice, not a feeling. When you choose love, you will continue to love even when the feelings are not there. If you have lost the feelings, the covenant remains. If by faith you will honor the covenant, you can press through the hard times and find that the feelings will return.

This love is at the heart of covenant living. You can honor the covenant-love relationship with people, even when you do not *feel* love. You can enter into a greater kind of love—the love of God. You are able to maintain a strong covenant life, regardless of others' actions or even their attacks.

God is love, and you have been born of love.

You must now choose to be ruled by love and give honor to the law of this Kingdom, the *royal law of love.*

The love life brings the rain of God's blessing and keeps you filled with the vision and hope of overcoming anything, because "love never fails" (1 Corinthians 13:8).

Serve God with all Your Heart

In Deuteronomy 11:13, God shows us another condition to create the atmosphere for rain: you must also "serve him with all your heart."

When Jesus became the Lord of your life, you became spiritually alive in your innermost being. Serving Him is more than just going through the right motions; now it can be a true spiritual service that flows freely from your heart and is pleasing to the Lord.

When the prophet Samuel was about to anoint a new king to replace Saul, he considered the sons of Jesse. One made a strong impression, and Samuel was sure this was the one who should be king. Then the Spirit of God spoke to Samuel.

Do not look at his appearance or at his

physical stature, because I have refused him. For the Lord does not see
as man sees; for man looks at the out-
ward appearance, but the Lord looks
at the heart (1 Samuel 16:7).

Later Jesse's youngest son, David, became
Israel's king—serving God and leading His people.
God could see in David a man after His own heart (1
Samuel 13:14).

You can learn to follow the leadership of the
Spirit that is within your own heart. God has made
you able to hear the voice of what Peter calls, "the
hidden person of the heart" (1 Peter 3:4).

When you serve God with your entire heart,
you are following His lead and His Word with a sincerity and commitment that will not be tossed by difficulties or attacks. You have decided to follow God,
even though others try to talk you out of it.

You have learned to guard your heart. Proverbs 4:23 says, "Keep your heart with all diligence,
for out of it spring the issues of life."

Within your heart is the reservoir of the blessing and virtue of God. Second Peter 1:3 says He has
given you "all things that pertain to life and godli-

ness." These forces of life flow out of your heart like a river when you release your faith and walk in the Word of God.

Jesus said in John 7:38, "He who believes in Me, as the Scripture has said, out of his heart will flow rivers of living water." He described the life of God in your heart as a river. You must tap into the resources of the Holy Spirit that He has placed within your inner man and begin to draw them out like water flowing.

There are waters of healing, abundance and freedom deposited within your heart. You can draw those waters out by faith.

There are waters of wisdom, counsel, understanding and discernment that you can learn to trust as you pursue God's will.

There are waters of love, joy and peace that will rule you and direct your steps.

You can become sure and steadfast by learning to serve God from your heart. You will be pleasing to Him as you serve Him with the sincerity and loyalty of undivided motives.

In Mark 4, Jesus taught that the Word of God sown into different kinds of ground would produce different results. He referred to one as "seed sown among thorns." This is ground that is *overcrowded.*

The overcrowded heart has many things growing. This heart has divided loyalties and divided desires. Though the ground has been fruitful, weeds and other unwanted plants can grow up and make the ground less and less productive.

Jesus' caution to us is very important. An overcrowded heart may be bearing some fruit, but it is well below its potential, because too many things have been allowed to enter.

The service that brings the rain is service with your *whole* heart. As you focus your desires upon God and His will for you, He can bring you into a place of still waters and green pastures—a place of tranquil provision.

Harmonize Your Thoughts and Purposes with Your Heart

The last part of Deuteronomy 11:13 says, "And serve Him...with all your soul." The soul is your mind, will and emotions. It is vital that your thoughts and purposes are in harmony with the desires of your heart.

One of the most important things you can do as a believer is to make the determined effort to renew your mind to begin to think the thoughts of God. You may ask, "How do you think God's thoughts?" You think the thoughts of God by causing your thoughts to agree with His Word.

Romans 12:2 says,

And do not be conformed to this world, but be transformed by the renewing of your mind, that you may prove what is that good and acceptable and perfect will of God.

The transformation of your life begins, and continues as you bring your thoughts into harmony with God's Word. Meditation in the Word is one of the ways you bring your thinking into line.

Romans 12:2 from the *J.B. Phillips* translation says, "Don't let the world around you squeeze you into its own mold, but let God remold your minds from within." You can let the Word change you from the inside out. Feed on God's thoughts until they are so much a part of you that they become your own thoughts.

The more you change within, the more the

Spirit of God has access to move in you and through you. He is totally committed to your success. Your commitment to obey, love and serve Him will make that success real.

God said,

"*Position yourselves*!"

When you take the right

position—standing in the

place He tells you—

you will overcome

the enemy.

Chapter Four

Positioned for God's Transfer of Wealth

God is looking for those who will demonstrate His goodness because they understand His purpose for wealth.

What hinders you from promoting the gospel more freely? Most likely, your answer, like that of most believers, would be a lack of money.

Most Christians have a deep desire to fund mission projects. They desire to help their churches or to join with ministries as prayer and financial partners.

The problem has been that the wealth of this world has been under the control of people who are promoting everything but the message of Jesus Christ.

How to Seize the Transfer of Wealth

Not long ago, three individual men gave away a combined total of $41 billion and not one dollar went to proclaim God's Word.

That's not God's plan. God's plan for wealth is that it be used for the promotion of His Kingdom—not for the promotion of another. He is moving in the hearts of the members of His family worldwide to take hold of wealth in order to demonstrate His goodness to those outside of His family.

Notice Psalm 31:19:

> Your goodness is so great! You have stored up great blessings for those who honor you. You have done so much for those who come to you for protection, blessing them before the watching world (*New Living Translation*).

Your increase and prosperity become a picture before a watching world. The world sees poverty on one side and greed and abuse on the other.

People are truly looking for those whose hearts are pure and whose motives can be trusted. You and I are to be the ones who receive and demonstrate God's goodness.

Romans 2:4 tells us that it is the goodness of God that brings people to repentance. God is calling the world to repent and know Him. And the Church must show the goodness of God on all levels of life.

Throughout biblical history God has brought abundant wealth to many of His people. When you begin to study it, the pattern becomes very evident.

God's Goodness Toward Abram

That pattern began with God's covenant partner Abram. He was made wealthy shortly after he began to walk with God. In a short time he received a great deal of wealth from the Pharaoh of Egypt because of Sarai, Abram's wife (see Genesis 12:16).

Genesis 13:2 says, "Abram was very rich in livestock, in silver, and in gold." Abram's wealth came out of Egypt and continued to grow, along with his power. His own men even conquered an alliance of five kings who had taken his nephew, Lot, captive.

Abram delivered the king of Sodom at the same time and offered the tithe of all the wealth he recovered to the priest and king, Melchizedek. Here the wealth of Sodom was brought into God's plan and purpose.

God's Goodness Toward Isaac

Abraham's son, Isaac, would also experience dramatic increase. The land in which Isaac lived suffered from a famine that had driven others living in the region to Egypt for help. But, at God's Word, Isaac remained in the land, risking everything. As a result he received one hundredfold on all of his crops.

Genesis 26:12-13 says,

That year Isaac's crops were tremendous! He harvested a hundred times more grain than he planted, for the Lord blessed him. He became a rich man, and his wealth only continued to grow *(New Living Translation)*.

God's Goodness Toward Jacob

Jacob, Isaac's son, received a plan from God that would transfer the wealth of his wicked father-in-law, Laban, into his possession. Jacob tended the flocks and herds of Laban for many years. Although Laban's wealth increased because of Jacob, Laban cheated Jacob. God showed Jacob how to turn this injustice around.

In Genesis 31:4-9, Jacob tells the details of

46

how this transfer took place.

> So Jacob sent and called Rachel and
> Leah to the field, to his flock, and said
> to them, "I see your father's counte-
> nance, that it is not favorable toward
> me as before; but the God of my fa-
> ther has been with me. And you know
> that with all my might I have served
> your father. Yet your father has de-
> ceived me and changed my wages ten
> times, but God did not allow him to
> hurt me. If he said thus: 'The speckled
> shall be your wages,' then all the
> flocks bore speckled. And if he said
> thus: 'The streaked shall be your
> wages,' then all the flocks bore
> streaked. So God has taken away the
> livestock of your father and given them
> to me."

Though Jacob served Laban with integrity,
Laban unfairly changed his wages ten times, but God
didn't allow Jacob to be hurt by his father-in-law. The
wealth of a wicked and unjust man was transferred
into the hands of a man who walked in covenant with
God.

God's Goodness Toward Joseph

One of Jacob's sons, Joseph, was used by God to bring the wealth of Egypt and other nations in that region to Israel. When Joseph received God-given dreams foretelling his future position of power, he was hated and betrayed by his own family.

By the end of his life he had been used by God to manage the greatest harvest and increase in Egypt's history. Joseph was the overseer of the harvest and the wealth that streamed into Egypt as other nations came to buy their grain.

All of that wealth was brought to Egypt because of Joseph. It never belonged to Egypt. Four hundred years later, when Israel left Egypt, God told them to go throughout the land and ask for gold, silver and clothing from each household. They departed with all that rightfully belonged to them—the wealth brought to the nation by Joseph's faith in God.

God's Goodness Toward Israel

In the end, Egypt paid this generation for all of the back wages the Israelites were due from four hundred years of labor.

Notice Psalm 105:37: "He also brought them

out with silver and gold, and there was none feeble among His tribes."

The *New Living Translation* states it this way:

But he brought his people safely out of Egypt, loaded with silver and gold; there were no sick or feeble people among them.

God's people were loaded! As long as they obeyed and trusted Him, the pattern of wealth and increase coming to them was clear. There are so many others. David, Israel's greatest king, led them into times of great victory and wealth. Solomon became the wisest and wealthiest man in all of history. He would have great wealth given to him from leaders, kings and queens of surrounding nations.

God's Goodness Toward Jehoshaphat

Another man had a remarkable experience of receiving the wealth of the world. In 2 Chronicles is the account of Jehoshaphat becoming king in Israel, and receiving an abundance of wealth. Yet, he nearly lost it all when he allied himself with the wicked king, Ahab.

His enemies were about to destroy him and all

of Israel when he called out to God and led the nation in repentance. When he did, God gave him clear direction that would deliver him and Israel from destruction.

In 2 Chronicles 20:17 we read the details,

You will not need to fight in this battle. Position yourselves, stand still and see the salvation of the Lord, who is with you, O Judah and Jerusalem! Do not fear or be dismayed; tomorrow go out against them, for the Lord is with you.

God said, *"Position yourselves!"* When you take the right position—standing in the place He tells you—you will overcome any enemy.

When they followed God's instructions, they saw Him destroy those who came to destroy them. What followed is beyond imagination:

When Jehoshaphat and his people came to take away their spoil, they found among them an abundance of valuables on the dead bodies, and precious jewelry, which they stripped off for themselves, more than they could carry away; and they were three

50

days gathering the spoil because there was so much (verse 25).

They spent three days collecting money and valuables. The wealth of their enemies was brought *to them*. All they had to do was gather it.

Pursue God's Plan

God has not changed. He will lead you in ways that will bring wealth and increase to you today. But there is an aspect that must be realized. In each of these examples, it was vital that they position themselves to obtain it. Abram obeyed, Isaac sowed, Jacob worked, Joseph refused to quit, Jehoshaphat set his heart right and walked with God. The result was that God blessed what each set his hand to achieve.

The wealth of the world is in the world not in church. God will give you plans and ideas to position you for increase. When you pursue His plan to achieve that increase, He has promised to do in you just what He has done in others. God will bless what you sow and what you set your hand to do, as you obey and walk with Him.

Today, God is raising up modern day testimonies of men and women who will become so abundantly rich that they may be vessels in His hand for distributing wealth and promoting the Word. You can be one of those He uses.

You can break the

limits and rise up to

a new level of receiving from

God. You can

turn your financial world

around and sever

the root of all evil once

and for all.

Chapter Five

Cutting the Root of
the Enemy's Power

The natural power of wealth has influenced every society from the very beginning. Money has been at the center of the rise and fall of every great empire. Whoever controlled the wealth could control governments and nations.

The god of this world has held on to the wealth in the earth with a clinched fist. He has manipulated and controlled multitudes through greed and materialism. He has gripped the earth's wealth as though it were all his—*but it is not*.

Psalm 24:1 says, "The earth is the Lord's, and all its fullness, the world and those who dwell therein."

All that is in the earth ultimately belongs to

God. Yet, He did not create it for Himself but for His family.

The time has come when God is moving the earth's wealth out of the control of the wicked and ungodly and into the hands of His family.

Satan's stronghold is about to be exposed and destroyed. The control of the earth's finances is shifting and being transferred into the hands of those who will honor God with it.

Among many religious people there has long been a sense that wealth was dangerous and certainly could not be spiritual. It has been blamed for corruption, compromise and the endangering of all that is holy.

Yet, wealth and money do not cause evil. Money only amplifies the inner qualities someone already possesses. If there are deep-rooted flaws, they will come to the surface and be seen. When a person has the money to do what he wants, you will find out what he really wanted all along.

If your heart is turned toward God, and His will is the desire of your heart, natural wealth will become the tool to amplify God's plan to move through you. Then these plans will move from being in your heart only to coming into your hands. The projects He has given people; the vision for ministry, land, equipment and all the other things needed to fulfill the calling of God can now be financed.

Satan's Final Stronghold

The fulfillment of all the callings and plans that God has planted in the hearts of His people has never been nearer than it is in our generation.

One day the Holy Spirit spoke some very startling words to me. He said, "This message of bringing wealth into the hands of believer's will tear down Satan's final stronghold." It struck my spirit like an explosion. He referred to this financial realm as a stronghold of Satan and the final stronghold God's family would overcome.

This opened up the question, "How can I understand this from the Word?" Anything we receive from the Spirit of God will completely agree with the Word.

The Holy Spirit pointed out that 1 Timothy 6:10 said, "For the love of money is the root of all evil" (*King James Version*). ALL EVIL! Every wicked and perverted thing has its root in the same thing—

the wrong concept of money. To love and regard wealth is to put it into a place of priority it does not belong.

This issue of money and wealth touches every aspect of evil Satan has ever designed against mankind. When we turn the money issue around and grasp its importance from a biblical standpoint, we will strike at the root of all of Satan's kingdom.

Money itself is not the root of evil, but the wrong attachment or affection for what wealth can do will open a person to Satan's strategies.

This means that every kind of evil has its root in the wrong use of wealth. Anything that has corrupted God's plan for man is evil. God did not bring mankind into sickness, pride, depression, fear, sexual perversions or poverty. These are all a result of man's separation from God through sin. They are manifestations of the sin that has twisted God's intentions for people.

Of course, a sick person is not necessarily evil. Nor is someone who is in poverty or depression. But his condition is a result of the pressure and plan Satan brings against all mankind. The thread, which links all of these wicked attacks together, is the love of money. Yes, the *love* of money.

Where is Your Focus?

The love of money is a focus on the wrong things.

When someone's focus is on natural things, it will keep that person from seeing with the right perspective. Anything money can buy is part of creation. The land, home, food, car or clothes bought with money are all natural things.

When a person sets his affections on these things, he has elevated them into a position in which they do not belong. When he makes his goal the pursuit of money, he has lifted the creation into the position reserved for the Creator.

Jesus said to "seek first the kingdom of God and His righteousness, and all these things shall be added to you" (Matthew 6:33). God alone is worthy to be sought.

Colossians 3:2 says it this way, "Set your mind on things above, not on things on the earth." Real wealth comes from fellowship with God. When your mind and affections remain on Him, you will keep your priorities in harmony with His will.

Knowing these things will turn the message of God's plan to prosper you into one of the most important things you could understand. This knowledge will strike at the root of every evil known to man.

What is a Stronghold?

To understand how God's people are going to strike this blow to the root of Satan's power, we need to make sure we understand what a stronghold is. A stronghold is a fortress, a place of strength.

Satan has used greed, covetousness and materialism to consume people with lust to divide them and turn them against one another. The strength of his kingdom is in deceiving people. If he can deceive them into making wealth the focus of their pursuits, then he can keep them limited to the natural realm and on the treadmill of never quite having enough.

A stronghold either holds people in or keeps them out. In one way, this stronghold of wrong thinking concerning wealth will keep people in the rat race of seeing and wanting but never being satisfied. It will keep them in natural and carnal thinking.

This same stronghold will keep people out of God's best.

Those Christians who remain carnal in their thinking will never find out how to rise up out of the worldly system of finance into God's way of doing things. They will never discover how to give in faith and receive from God. They may give but not grasp the importance of increasing. They will be limited to what they can do naturally.

Cut the Root and Destroy the Fruit

You can break the limits and rise up to a new level of receiving from God. You can turn your financial world around and sever the root of all evil once and for all.

The importance of attacking this financial arena is that if you can cut the root of every evil designed against mankind, you can destroy the fruit. When money is in its proper priority, it will be used but not abused. It will do what it was designed to do—glorify God.

Wealth is for the purpose and plan of God. His plan is for you to prosper personally, promote the gospel of Jesus and bring freedom to people worldwide. His purpose is to destroy the works of the devil. What better way to destroy his work than to take from him the wealth he has considered his.

How to Seize the Transfer of Wealth

You can become a vital part of God's plan to transfer the wealth that is still in the world system. Let this check list help you tear down Satan's final stronghold:

- First, know that all wealth is for God's plan and purpose.

- Second, commit yourself to His plan to prosper you.

- Third, recognize the pitfalls of improper priorities.

- Fourth, set your mind and affections on His goals and priorities.

- Fifth, give tithes and offerings in faith expecting to receive.

- Sixth, expect ideas and insights that will keep increase and prosperity coming toward you.

- Seventh, be thankful for what you now have and all He has blessed you with.

God is committed to bring His increase to you and destroy all that Satan has done to pervert His plans for people. You can rise up, cut the root of the enemy's power and receive all that God has for you.

"He increased His people greatly, and made them stronger than their enemies" (Psalm 105:24).

Whatever you do

to make God's dream

in others become

reality—God will do to

make His dream in you

become reality.

Chapter Six

Move Toward Your Dream by Blessing the Blessed

God first spoke to Abram that through covenant He would establish an entrance into every nation on earth. God was moving to bring His dream of blessing mankind into reality, and He needed a man to start with.

Abram, who would later be called Abraham, is the father of faith, and he is called the father of us all. It was his faith in God's Word that changed everything. The covenant he entered into made God's blessing and abundance available to anyone who would pursue the God of Abraham.

Notice Genesis 12:1-3 where God first speaks to Abraham:

Now the Lord had said to Abram: 'Get

out of your country, from your family and from your father's house, to a land that I will show you. I will make you a great nation; I will bless you and make your name great; and you shall be a blessing. I will bless those who bless you, and I will curse him who curses you; and in you all the families of the earth shall be blessed.'

The Amplified Bible sheds important light on verse 3:

And I will bless those who bless you [who confer prosperity or happiness upon you] and curse him who curses or uses insolent language toward you; in you will all the families and kindred of the earth be blessed [and by you they will bless themselves].

People bless themselves when they bless the blessed. This is a law of God which needs to be explored.

Those who would confer prosperity or happiness on Abram would bring upon themselves the blessing which God placed on him.

66

This law will work for you too. You will bring blessing and prosperity on yourself by finding men and women of God who are walking in their covenant of blessing and joining with them by blessing them. When you give to those who are receiving from God with success, you can enter into their success and also begin to receive for yourself.

To use the words of *The Amplified Bible*, those upon whom you confer prosperity and happiness will be blessed by God, bringing blessing on yourself.

The word *bless* is interesting. It's meaning includes "to empower to prosper." When you confer prosperity through your giving, you empower another to prosper. When you bless another, you also bless yourself.

It is a misconception to think that the only kind of generosity God is expecting of us is toward the poor. Without question we are to give to those who are less fortunate. However, government assistance has demonstrated that giving financial help without teaching people how to come out of lack and poverty is never going to answer the problem.

The real issue of poverty is spiritual. You must

get poverty out of a person in order to keep a person out of poverty.

The Link to Blessing

There were people around Jesus who did not understand His view of this exact truth. We see this in the account of a lavish offering given to Jesus:

> Then, six days before the Passover, Jesus came to Bethany, where Lazarus was who had been dead, whom He had raised from the dead. There they made Him a supper; and Martha served, but Lazarus was one of those who sat at the table with Him.
>
> Then Mary took a pound of very costly oil of spikenard, anointed the feet of Jesus, and wiped His feet with her hair. And the house was filled with the fragrance of the oil.
>
> Then one of His disciples, Judas Iscariot, Simon's son, who would betray Him, said, "Why was this fragrant oil not sold for three hundred denarii and given to the poor?" This he said not that he cared for the poor, but be-

cause he was a thief, and had the money box; and he used to take what was put in it.

But Jesus said, "Let her alone; she has kept this for the day of My burial. For the poor you have with you always, but Me you do not have always" (John 12:1-8).

This offering was given to Jesus by Mary, the sister to Lazarus. The value was equal to an average worker's salary for an entire year. This was a wealthy woman who gave an extravagant and seemingly unreasonable offering directly to Jesus. It was not something He needed, yet He still received it.

The disciples, however, criticized her sharply for her extravagance. They considered it a waste to pour out this expensive oil on Jesus.

Judas took his criticism to another level. He said this should have been sold and given to the poor. His motive was not his love for the poor. He was a thief, and his heart was governed by dishonesty.

This same criticism can be heard today, and for the same reason. Carnal-minded people fail to see the value of giving to ministries and ministers of God. It is viewed as a waste and manipulation.

Yet, the same motive that Judas revealed governs their hearts also. They may not be stealing from the offerings, but they are thieves by failing to honor God with their own offerings.

Jesus did not view this extravagant offering as a waste but rather as a spiritual offering from Mary's heart. It would also link her to her own blessing. She had honored a law of God.

Let Blessing Rest on Your House

The prophet Ezekiel shed further light on this concept. Notice Ezekiel 44:30:

> The best of all firstfruits of any kind, and every sacrifice of any kind from all your sacrifices, shall be the priest's; also you shall give to the priest the first of your ground meal, to cause a blessing to rest on your house.

He said their giving would cause blessing to rest on their houses when they gave the priests the best of their firstfruits.

Proverbs 3:9-10 goes on to give details about

how this blessing would come:

> Honor the Lord with your possessions, and with the firstfruits of all your increase; so your barns will be filled with plenty, and your vats will overflow with new wine.

Filled with plenty and overflowing! God is looking for ways to bring His overflow and abundance into your life. He wants there to be such a supply of wealth and every good thing that it is flowing out from you in every direction. His way is for you to be a resource of increase to others. *Whatever you do to make God's dream in others become reality, God will do to make His dream in you become reality.*

Every person must learn the system God has given to us. It is to enter into the abundance of God by giving and blessing those who are blessed of God. Both the work of ministry, and the worker are worthy to be blessed.

Jesus tells you exactly what can be expected when you obey Him and give. Luke 6:38 says,

> Give, and it will be given to you: good measure, pressed down, shaken together, and running over will be put

into your bosom. For with the same measure that you use, it will be measured back to you.

You can expect more to come back to you than what you gave away.

Another example of blessing the blessed is found in the life of Job. He was the richest man in the east before Satan's attack against him. When Job remained faithful to God in the midst of every attack, there was nothing Satan could do to prevent Job from increasing. The result was that Job was blessed with twice as much as he previously owned.

Now notice what happened in Job 42:10-11:

And the Lord restored Job's losses when he prayed for his friends. Indeed the Lord gave Job twice as much as he had before. Then all his brothers, all his sisters, and all those who had been his acquaintances before, came to him and ate food with him in his house; and they consoled him and comforted him for all the adversity that the Lord had brought upon him. Each one gave him a piece of silver and each a ring of gold.

Though he was the richest man in the east, and now possessed twice as much as before, they were compelled to give him gold and silver. They blessed the blessed.

The parable Jesus taught in Matthew 25 regarding the three servants each receiving talents of money when their lord was going away is very clear. Upon the lord's return, the one servant who had only kept his one talent had it taken away from him and given to the one who possessed ten talents. The one who needed it least was the one to whom the Lord gave it.

Sowing Into Fruitful Soil

If we limit our giving to only those who look like they are in need, we have turned a deaf ear to the voice of the Holy Spirit. The ministry that is growing financially is blessed of God. If I choose to send my support to one who is struggling *because* he is struggling, I am being led by my feelings and reasoning. That is simply carnal thinking.

There has been limited understanding of what a *need* actually is which has contributed to a great deal of misunderstanding in giving. Paul said, "And my God shall supply all your need according to His riches in glory by Christ Jesus" (Philippians 4:19).

How to Seize the Transfer of Wealth

Contrary to what most think, needs are not what it takes to merely exist. Some have thought their needs would be met if they owned a house, an automobile or enough money to pay their bills. God's view of your need, however, is not based on you but on His calling for your life.

When God speaks to you about your life, He will actually *create* a need. One Word from God gives you a need. He will give you a vision for something that you could never do on your own. Suddenly, you need His supernatural supply to fulfill His plans and direction. But along with direction for His will comes His grace to supply the need in full with His abundant supply.

The Holy Spirit is moving His Body out of carnal thinking which has been led by need and feeling. No longer will we be led by manipulation and guilt in our giving. He is leading us from giving out of need into seeing from His point of view to bless those He is blessing.

God will speak to you to do the unreasonable in order to move you into the unlimited realm of the supernatural. It may seem unreasonable to your natural way of thinking, but you are no longer limited to the natural point of view. God wants you to be free to see things from His point of view.

When you find someone who is blessed and being a blessing to others, sow your seeds of prayer and finances into that field, and in doing so you will be blessing yourself.

God is the great giver.

He so loved that He gave.

Yet, God gave with

purpose—He expected

to receive back more

than He gave. He gave His

Son and would receive many

sons. His giving was the

means to a greater end.

Chapter Seven

The Power to Prosper
in All Things

Look up on a clear night.

Seeing the estimated 6,000 stars visible on the clearest night is all you need to realize God does things in a big way. And even the magnificence of that is not the whole picture. Science has discovered many millions of stars—far more than what can be seen.

It's just one proof of the fact that God never does only enough to satisfy the situation; He always provides *more* than enough. From turning water into wine to feeding thousands on a hillside, God always provides more than what was necessary. He is the God of abundance.

A knowing that God wants to abundantly provide for us is within the heart of every believer. He wants to be Lord of all and is ready to show His love, power and provision to humanity. God is able and willing to demonstrate His loving and giving nature to all of His children.

To clearly see God's will stated, we need only to look at 3 John 1:2, "Beloved, I pray that you may prosper in all things and be in health, just as your soul prospers."

This verse leaves no question that God wants us to prosper in all things. He has given us the power to receive from Him through faith. But if we are to prosper in all things properly, it is vital that our eyes be on Him and not on natural things.

Knowing God as Our Only Source

If our trust is misdirected and resting on natural things instead of the laws of abundance, we will never rise up in His power to prosper. Jesus made this truth clear one day when a rich young man came to Him. This account is found in Mark 10:17-22:

> Now as He was going out on the road, one came running, knelt before Him, and asked Him, "Good Teacher, what shall I do that I may inherit eternal life?"

So Jesus said to him, "Why do you call Me good? No one is good but One, that is, God. You know the commandments: 'Do not commit adultery,' 'Do not murder,' 'Do not steal,' 'Do not bear false witness,' 'Do not defraud,' 'Honor your father and your mother.'"

And he answered and said to Him, "Teacher, all these I have observed from my youth."

Then Jesus, looking at him, loved him, and said to him, "One thing you lack: Go your way, sell whatever you have and give to the poor, and you will have treasure in heaven; and come, take up the cross, and follow Me."

But he was sad at this word, and went away sorrowful, for he had great possessions.

This young man lacked the understanding of the power of giving. He followed God's laws for his spiritual relationship, but in natural things his trust was in his wealth. Jesus wanted to teach him to trust God in natural things as well as spiritual. The man was familiar with the commandments and had lived by the law of Moses. He had a heart hungry to know God, but he needed to grasp a new aspect of God's desire for people. It was an area he never realized God was interested in to this degree. God wants to be our source of supply on every level.

Stop Earth-Bound Thinking

Jesus was pulling this man out of his earth-bound, natural thinking. To give on the level Jesus asked was not natural. He would have to let go of everything he had known and trust God's promises for natural, as well as spiritual blessings.

Some have interpreted Jesus' comments to mean He required the young man to become poor before he could follow Him. But Jesus was not suggesting a person must be poor to follow Him. Proverbs 19:17 says, "He who has pity on the poor lends to the Lord, and He will pay back what he has given."

Jesus knew that if this man gave to the poor, God would pay him back just as the Word promised. He would not remain poor, and the wealth that came to him would be the result of God's promises and not human effort. This man would be living proof that God was even God over his money.

View Giving as Gain—Not Loss

The problem was that this young man's thinking was still tied to his wealth. Instead of trusting Jesus and obeying Him, he walked away from Jesus sad. His sadness was due to his wrong perspective. He saw his giving as a loss and not a gain.

When we only see giving in the light of having less, we have missed God's purpose in our giving. Giving our money is our link to bringing God's provision into our lives. It unlocks the windows of heaven and brings God into every financial part of our lives.

God is the great giver. He so loved that He gave. Yet, God gave with purpose; He expected to receive back more than He gave. He gave His Son and would receive many sons. His giving was the means to a greater end.

The great evangelist F. F. Bosworth said, "The only purpose of God's promises is their fulfillment."

God's purpose in promising to prosper you is so that He can fulfill His Word. First Kings 8:56 says, "There has not failed one word of all His good promises." He is committed to His Word. Jeremiah 1:12 says He watches over His Word to perform it.

Promises Regarding Prosperity

Notice God's promises regarding prosperity:

♦ "And my God shall supply all your
   need according to His riches in
   glory by Christ Jesus" (Philippians
   4:19). He will supply your needs on
   every level including natural and
   financial.

When God's people were delivered from generations of slavery in Egypt they came out with
wealth and health.

♦ Psalm 105:37 says, "He also
   brought them out with silver and
   gold, and there was none feeble
   among His tribes."

♦ To the one whose heart delights in
   the Word, Psalm 112:3 says,
   "Wealth and riches will be in his
   house, and his righteousness en-
   dures forever."

♦ Job 36:11 says, "If they obey and
   serve Him, they shall spend their
   days in prosperity, and their years
   in pleasures."

Positioned for the Supernatural

God spoke to the prophet Elijah and sent him to the city of Zarephath, a Phoenician city whose religion included the worship of the false gods Baal and Ashtoreth. It was here that God would use a widow to provide for him.

> So he arose and went to Zarephath. And when he came to the gate of the city, indeed a widow was there gathering sticks. And he called to her and said, "Please bring me a little water in a cup, that I may drink." And as she was going to get it, he called to her and said, "Please bring me a morsel of bread in your hand." So she said, "As the Lord your God lives, I do not have bread, only a handful of flour in a bin, and a little oil in a jar; and see, I am gathering a couple of sticks that I may go in and prepare it for myself and my son, that we may eat it, and die." And Elijah said to her, "Do not fear; go and do as you have said, but make me a small cake from it first, and bring it to me; and afterward make some for

yourself and your son. For thus says the Lord God of Israel: 'The bin of flour shall not be used up, nor shall the jar of oil run dry, until the day the Lord sends rain on the earth.'"

So she went away and did according to the word of Elijah; and she and he and her household ate for many days. The bin of flour was not used up, nor did the jar of oil run dry, according to the word of the Lord which He spoke by Elijah (1 Kings 17:10-16).

Her willingness to give to the man of God positioned her for God to do something supernatural. When you provide the *natural*, God provides the *super* and you receive His *supernatural*.

It seemed so unreasonable for Elijah to ask her for anything. She was in a desperate situation herself. She saw no future for her or her son—only that they would eat their last cake and die.

She had to look beyond the immediate and believe there was more.

Elijah had come to bring provision to her and her son, but first she would have to give to the man of God. The very things she used to make the cake, the flour and oil, were what God multiplied.

She had acted on one of the divine laws of abundance without even realizing it. Again, in Luke 6:38 Jesus said,

> Give, and it will be given to you: good measure, pressed down, shaken together, and running over will be put into your bosom. For with the same measure that you use, it will be measured back to you.

The way this law of God works is that you choose the measure when you give and God will begin to bring increase back to you in that measure. You have the right to prosper in all that you do. The power released when you give in faith will unlock abundant provision and power for you to prosper.

> Let them shout for joy and be glad, who favor my righteous cause; and let them say continually, 'Let the Lord be magnified, who has pleasure in the prosperity of His servant' (Psalm 35:27).

Dennis Burke is affecting thousands of people worldwide. At the heart of this ministry is a focus on faith in the Word of God and an inner desire to walk in the power and the flow of the Holy Spirit—this explosive combination will keep the fire of God burning in His people.

Beginning as an associate pastor and youth minister in Southern California, Dennis received great insight into the work of the local church. In 1976, he and his wife, Vikki, moved to Fort Worth, Texas to work with Kenneth Copeland Ministries. Two years later, God led him to enter his own ministry. Since that time, Dennis has continued his involvement with Kenneth Copeland Ministries as a guest speaker for the *Believers' Voice of Victory* broadcast, the *Believers' Conventions* and annual *Ministers' Conference*. Dennis' articles have been featured in the *Believers' Voice of Victory* magazine.

Dennis' ministry takes him to a different part of the United States every week, as well as Australia, Asia, New Zealand, Canada, Sweden, France, Ukraine and South Africa. Dennis has authored several books including *How to Meditate God's Word* which has been translated into Spanish, Russian and

Tagalog.

In addition, he serves as President for the *International Convention of Faith Ministries* (ICFM) and is a featured speaker at National and International conventions. Dennis has brought answers to many, continuing to strive for excellence in ministry.

The *People of Promise* Are Impacting Lives!

Reports come in daily from people around the world who are being changed by the power of God's Word through Dennis Burke Ministries—about how God's Word has brought healing, hope, restoration to a marriage or salvation to a loved one.

Our Partners are a vital part of all the work we are doing. Every person who is changed through this ministry will have our Partners to thank. Our Partners—the *People of Promise* are those who have joined with this ministry through their monthly financial giving to help fulfill the Great Commission.

When you join in Partnership, the anointing, favor and grace that rests on this ministry will rest upon you. When you have a need in your family, your business, your finances or whatever it might be, you can draw upon the anointing that operates in this ministry to help.

Also, as a Partner you will never be without prayer! Dennis and Vikki, as well as their staff pray for you. When you send your prayer requests we join our faith with yours for the anointing of God to remove every burden and destroy every yoke!

Even though our calling is to the world, our hearts are devoted to our Partners. That's why we have designed a Collector's Series exclusively for our Partners—*People of Promise.*

The Collector's Series gives our Partners the opportunity each month to receive an exclusive teaching tape in which we teach a Word in season and pray for you.

When you send your first offering of $20.00 or more, you will receive a beautiful Collector's Series album and the first tape in the series. Each time you send your monthly offering, you can request the next tape in the series.

Join the *People of Promise* family today! Simply fill out the coupon on the following page and enclose your initial partnership offering. We will receive you as our Partner and pray for God's best to be multiplied to you now!

Tear out the coupon and mail to: Dennis Burke Ministries, PO Box 150043, Arlington, TX 76015.

I want to join Dennis and Vikki in fulfilling the Great Commission. Enclosed is my first offering to establish my monthly partnership.

☐ $100　☐ $50　　☐ $20　　☐ $_____
　　　　　　　　　　　　　　　　　　(Other)

☐ Please send my Collector's Series album and my first tape.

Name _____

Address _____

City_____

State _____ Zip _____

Phone (_____) _____

VISA or MasterCard Number:

_____

Expiration Date: _____

(B17)

For a complete list of all books, audio
and video cassettes by
Dennis and Vikki Burke
or to receive their free publication,
Words to the Wise,
write:

Dennis Burke Ministries
PO Box 150043
Arlington, TX 76015
(817) 277-9627

*Feel free to include your prayer requests when
you write.*

Visit our website at:
www.dennisburkeministries.org
E-mail address: dbmin@aol.com

BOOKS BY DENNIS BURKE

*Dreams Really Do Come
True—It Can Happen to You!*
B16 – $12.95

Develop A Winning Attitude
B13 – $2.00

Breaking Financial Barriers
B12 – $5.00

You Can Conquer Life's Conflicts
B06 – $5.99

Grace: Power Beyond Your Ability
B07 – $5.99

* How to Meditate God's Word
B01 – $5.99

* Available in Spanish
B08 – $5.99

Knowing God Intimately
B04 – $5.99

The Law of the Wise
B02 – $5.99

VIDEO TAPES BY
DENNIS BURKE

Our Covenant of Increase
V108 – $15.00

Closing the Doors to the Enemy
V107 – $15.00

How to Obtain the Unobtainable
V109 – $15.00

Taking Charge of Your Future
V110 – $15.00

Ingredients to Increasing the Anointing
V111 – $15.00

Get Ready—His Glory is Rising Up in You
V112 – $15.00

You Can Bring What God Has in Heaven onto Earth
V113 – $15.00

How to Apply the Laws that
Bring Success
V106 – $15.00
B02 – $5.99

BOOKS BY VIKKI BURKE

Aim Your Child Like An Arrow
B10 – $5.00

Relief and Refreshing
B11 – $2.00

The Power of Peace—Protection and Direction
B14 – $2.00

AUDIO TAPES BY
VIKKI BURKE

Pressing Through the Promise into Possession
DBM50 Three tape series $15.00

Burn with Passion—Reach a Higher Level of Living
DBM56 Two tape set $10.00

Relief and Refreshing
DBM49 Two tape set $10.00

VIDEO TAPES BY
VIKKI BURKE

God Likes Things Hot!
V114 – $15.00